GROWING SUCCULENTS FOR BEGINNERS

A BEGINNERS STEP BY STEP GUIDE ON GROWING SUCCULENTS

CHANCE MOUSER

Table of Contents

CHAPTER ONE

GROWING SUCCULENTS

Incorporating succulents into the landscape is an exotic and eye-catching way to enhance the look of your garden, whether in the form of an eye-catching rock garden, an eye-catching container arrangement, or even an outdoor artwork. Succulents, on the other hand, are hardy and adaptable, preferring neglect to constant care.

Succulents have the added benefit of not requiring a green thumb to successfully grow. With minimal intervention, your succulents will thrive and even self-proliferate if you mimic their natural habitats. Tom Jesch, an expert at Waterwise Botanicals, has put together a list of eight tips for getting your succulent garden off to a strong start. Gardening with succulents is a truly unique experience. The glaucous, fleshy leaves of the evergreens add a different kind of texture to a garden scene.

A wide variety of species and geographical origins are represented by the numerous genera of succulents. One thing they all have in common is the ability to go long periods of time without drinking any water. These plants are native to dry, arid areas, including deserts where rain is scarce. This means that they require very little watering and can thrive in low-maintenance landscapes.

Sedums, sempervivums, agaves, aeoniums, and string of pearls are popular succulents. All of them are grown for their foliage rather than their flowering qualities.. Houseplants can also benefit from the presence of succulents.

Protecting succulents from extreme temperatures is a first step.

Only a few succulent varieties can withstand temperatures below freezing, so plan ahead if you want to grow them outside. Some desert environments can be too harsh for even the most tolerant of succulents. According to Jesch, "there are exceptions." Sempervivums and sedums (alpine species) can withstand temperatures as low as -70°F. A variety of succulents can survive in the extreme heat, including agaves, some aloes, and nearly all cacti.

Succulents that can be left outside all year round in mild climates are easy to come by. Planting hens and chicks is recommended by Jesch. There are many different kinds of Elephant's Food (Portulacaria afra) and Aeonium "Plum Petals" as well as the Echeveria

"Sahara," Agave "Moonshine," Crassula "Ripple Jade," and "Hobbit Jade."

Make sure they don't get too much exposure to sunlight.

A common misconception among first-time succulent gardeners is that their plants will thrive best in full sun, but this isn't always the case. Among the thousands of varieties of succulents, there is a wide range of preferences." Some prefer the shade, while others prefer filtered light, while still others prefer full-on sun.

CHAPTER TWO

According to Jesch, "the majority of people prefer two to three hours of sun or filtered sun each day."

A window or a garden room in full sun for at least two or three hours a day is ideal for growing succulents indoors. Succulents can be overwintered under grow lights if a sunny window isn't an option. To avoid sunburn, Jesch recommends re-introducing your plants to the outdoors gradually once they are able to enjoy outdoor conditions again.

When it comes to succulents, water is essential.

Watering your succulents on a regular basis, especially during the active growing season, is not going to kill them. Waiting for the soil to dry out between waterings is essential in order to allow the roots to breathe. Every few days to every two to three weeks during cool or low-light seasons, depending on the weather, time of year, pot size, and soil conditions in your garden." "I've seen many succulents survive for several months without water," says Jesch.

Just by looking at them, can you tell if they are getting enough water? To tell if a plant is healthy, look at its leaves. Your succulents' leaves will look shriveled and lackluster if they're thirsty. Stem or root rot and mushy or yellowing leaves are symptoms of overwatering.

. Make sure the soil and sand are the proper proportions.

Because succulent roots dislike sitting in wet soil, it's critical that you amend your soil with sand or pumice before planting. Perlite, small gravel, crushed granite, and Turface are all non-organic materials that can aid in loosening the soil (a calcined clay product).

"To prevent the soil from becoming too heavy, we prefer to use volcanic sands (pumice and scoria), but regular sand works just fine. Because of concerns about shipping weight, most commercial mixes are deficient in sand. According to

Jesch, about 60% nonorganic and 40% organic material provides good drainage and long-term stability.

After planting, do not backfill.

You should dig a hole big enough to accommodate the root ball when planting succulents in a garden. Leave the plant alone!" Keep the soil away from the roots, as Jesch advises.

Leaving this space between the soil and the roots allows the soil to gradually re-enter around the roots at the same rate as the plant grows. This encourages the growth of new roots near the surface of the soil, where they can receive oxygen from the air.. When it comes to cultivating succulents, Jesch has a few tips for you.

Soil with a lot of organic material mixed in or tilled near the roots of most succulents is not ideal. "Avoid mounding mulch near the crown or base of succulents if using mulch." In order to avoid sitting on or collaring the plant, Jesch recommends reducing or removing some distance from it. Crushed rock, granite, or decorative stone can be used as a non-biodegradable mulch. Soil drying and eroding will be prevented by using these mulches.

Put them in containers.

For those who can't keep their succulent plants outside all year, it's best to keep them in containers so that they can be moved indoors or to a more protected area when the weather changes. Haworthia, Gasteria, crown of thorns (Euphorbia millii), Easter lily cactus (Echinopsis), Sanseveria, and Christmas cactus are some of the succulents that will thrive on a sunny windowsill (Zygocactus).

Leaving an air gap isn't as important when planting in pots, according to Jesch, as long as the pot drains well and the plants aren't planted too deeply. Use a quick-draining soil mix in the same way you would in the ground. To improve drainage in potting soil, you can add fine sand or gravel to it.

Wait at least two or three days before thoroughly watering your succulents, according to Jesch's advice. To prevent root rot, allow the roots to rest before they soak up water. To remove salts and oxygen from the water, he says, "it's also important that the container has enough drainage holes to allow the water to drain through, wash out salts, and exchange."

CHAPTER THREE

If your succulents are getting out of control, don't be afraid to shape or prune them, especially if there are several of them together. Keep one variety from overpowering the other by doing this

"Tipping, clipping, branch removal, and dividing are all acceptable methods of trimming." According to Jesch, cuttings from pruning can either be replanted or given away. Allow the cuttings to dry and heal at the wound for a few days before planting to avoid them absorbing too much water during the growing process.

Remove any dry or dead leaves from the plant's base and surrounding area on a regular basis, too. Lower and outer leaves on succulents naturally fall off as they mature. Besides enhancing the appearance of your plants, removing the shriveled foliage encourages new growth and increases air circulation.

. Make sure they get enough to eat.

The shallow root systems of succulents and cacti necessitate that they be fertilized on a regular basis. A lack of fertilizer causes succulents to yellow and die, as well as lose their lovely luster and vibrant foliage colors that make them so beloved, according to Jesch.

After planting succulents in the garden, he suggests using an all-purpose 15-15-15 fertilizer, which should be applied within a couple of weeks and then repeated two or three times a year. Apply a general-purpose houseplant fertilizer once a month to potted succulents.

How to Use Succulent Plants in Your Garden in Five Different Ways

• Plant succulents closely together in a pattern to create a tapestry. To create a living work of art, use plants of all colors and shapes as your embroidery materials.

• Plant a succulent arrangement that resembles sea creatures or plants to recreate the exotic underwater world. See Waterwise Botanicals' selection of "seascape" plants for inspiration.

Natural stone or stone-like containers can be used in place of a traditional rock garden to create the illusion that succulents are emerging from a rock outcropping.

Incorporating succulents into living walls and vertical gardens is an effective way to showcase an array of succulent colors, shapes and textures. Create your own succulent wall in your back yard by following these instructions.

Plant succulents in letter-shaped frames made of old pallet or fence wood to create a succulent letter garden. First and last names can be used, but you can also spell out words and phrases. When writing letters with curves, bear this in mind: they are more difficult to form.

Try these succulent varieties!

THE END